Animals of the World

The Giant Pandas of China

by Jane Duden

Content Consultant:
Don Middleton
Member, International Association for
Bear Research and Management

Hilltop Books

An Imprint of Franklin Watts
A Division of Grolier Publishing
New York London Hong Kong Sydney
Danbury, Connecticut

Hilltop Books
http://publishing.grolier.com
Copyright © 1998 by Capstone Press • All rights reserved
Published simultaneously in Canada • Printed in the United States of America

Library of Congress Cataloging-in-Publication Data
Duden, Jane.
    The giant pandas of China / by Jane Duden.
        p. cm. -- (Animals of the world)
    Includes bibliographical references and index.
    Summary: Introduces the world of giant pandas, their physical
characteristics, behavior, and interaction with humans.
    ISBN 1-56065-577-1
    1. Giant panda--Juvenile literature.   [1. Giant panda.
2. Pandas.] I. Title. II. Series.
QL737C214D824   1998   97-11369
599.789--dc21   CIP
                                                AC

Photo credits
Heather Angel, 4, 6, 12, 14, 16
Charles Crust, 8
Lynn M. Stone, cover, 10, 18, 20

Table of Contents

About Giant Pandas 5

What Giant Pandas Look Like 7

Where Giant Pandas Live 9

What Giants Pandas Do 11

Giant Panda Enemies and Dangers 13

Mating and Reproduction 15

Newborn and Young Giant Pandas 17

Bamboo and Giant Pandas 19

Giant Pandas and People 21

Fast Facts 22

Words to Know 23

Read More 23

Useful Addresses 24

Internet Sites 24

Index 24

About Giant Pandas

Giant pandas are mammals. A mammal is a warm-blooded animal that has a backbone. Warm-blooded means that an animal's body is always the same temperature. Temperature is how hot or cold something is. Baby mammals drink milk from their mothers' bodies.

Giant pandas belong to the bear family of animals. Scientists once disagreed about what kind of mammal the giant panda is. But most scientists now place giant pandas in the bear family.

Wild giant pandas live only in bamboo forests in China. Bamboo is the giant panda's main food. Bamboo is a tall grass with a tough stem. Panda means bamboo eater in Nepal. Nepal is a country near China in Asia. Giant pandas once lived there.

Adult male giant pandas are about five to six feet (more than 1.5 meters) long. This measure is from their heads to their tails. They weigh between 175 and 275 pounds (80 and 125 kilograms). Females are a little smaller than males.

Most scientists think giant pandas belong to the bear family.

What Giant Pandas Look Like

Giant pandas have thick white and black fur. Their large heads are covered with white fur. Black fur covers their ears and circles their eyes. Black fur covers all four legs. Giant pandas' fur is very thick.

Giant pandas walk on all four feet. Each foot has five toes. A short, curved claw sticks out of each toe. Giant pandas use their claws to pull bamboo plants from the ground. They also use their claws to protect themselves.

Giant pandas' front feet have a special part. These are called panda's thumbs, but they are not thumbs. A panda's thumb is a long part of a giant panda's wristbone. Each front foot has a panda's thumb. They help giant pandas grip bamboo with their feet.

Giant pandas walk on all four feet.

Where Giant Pandas Live

Wild giant pandas live only in the mountains of western China. The weather there is cold and damp. It rains often. Bamboo grows well in these mountains. Giant pandas live in the high mountains in summer. In winter, they move to lower mountains.

Giant pandas live on the ground. They find shelter in bad weather. They use caves or hollow trees. Giant pandas do not usually build nests. But female giant pandas build nests before giving birth.

Giant pandas live alone except when mating or caring for young. Each giant panda has its own range. A range is the area where an animal lives. A giant panda's range is about one and a half to two and a half square miles (four to six square kilometers).

Giant pandas live in the mountains of western China.

What Giant Pandas Do

Giant pandas spend about 16 hours a day eating. They eat mainly the leaves and stems of bamboo plants. Giant pandas sometimes eat other plants, small animals, or fish.

Giant pandas must eat large amounts of bamboo. A giant panda's body does not have much time to digest the bamboo. Digest means to break down food so the body can use it. Pandas digest food quickly. Each giant panda eats between 22 and 84 pounds (10 and 38 kilograms) of bamboo a day.

Giant pandas move slowly through the forest. They rest when they are not eating. They sit against a tree or lie on the ground to rest.

Giant pandas are quiet most of the time. But they can make many different sounds. They make a sound like a sheep as a friendly greeting. They clack their teeth and smack their lips when they are scared. An angry giant panda growls or roars.

Giant pandas must eat large amounts of bamboo.

Giant Panda Enemies and Dangers

Giant pandas have only a few natural predators. A predator is an animal that hunts other animals for food. Leopards and wild dogs sometimes hunt giant pandas. Then giant pandas run away or climb a tree. Sometimes they fight back with their teeth and claws.

Leopards and wild dogs do not kill adult giant pandas very often. But predators do kill young giant pandas. They attack when female giant pandas are away from their young.

People are the greatest danger to giant pandas. Many giant pandas die in traps people set for other animals. Some giant pandas are killed by hunters. The government of China made laws against killing giant pandas. But some people want to buy giant panda skins. So hunting still goes on.

People also hurt giant pandas by destroying their food and homes. People cut down bamboo plants to make room for houses and farms. Then there is not enough food for the giant pandas.

Leopards sometimes hunt giant pandas.

Mating and Reproduction

Giant pandas mate during spring. Mate means to join together to produce young. Giant pandas are ready to mate when they are six to seven years old.

Males start looking for females to mate with. They bark and roar to let the females know they are ready. Giant pandas also mark trees. They rub their bodies against the trees. Liquid from their bodies comes off on the trees. This leaves a scent on the trees. It tells other giant pandas that a giant panda is ready to mate.

Females and males stay together for one to three days. After mating, giant pandas go back to living alone. A female finds a safe place or builds a nest. The female gives birth to a cub 14 to 23 weeks after mating. She will mate again in 18 to 24 months.

Male pandas rub their bodies against trees when they are ready to mate.

Newborn and Young Giant Pandas

A newborn giant panda is called a cub. A giant panda cub weighs about four ounces (112 grams). It has almost no hair and cannot see. The mother holds the cub all the time. The cub mostly sleeps and drinks milk from its mother.

The cub's eyes open after six weeks. It then learns to crawl. The mother can now leave her cub while she looks for food. After 10 weeks, the cub can stand and take a few steps. After three months, the cub is two feet (60 centimeters) long. It weighs 12 pounds (five and one half kilograms).

A cub learns to walk when it is about six months old. It begins to eat bamboo and climb trees. A young giant panda leaves its mother when it is 18 to 24 months old. It goes off to find its own range.

A cub learns to walk when it is about six months old.

Bamboo and Giant Pandas

Giant pandas eat 15 kinds of bamboo in the mountains of China. Each kind of bamboo goes through a die-off every 40 to 100 years. A die-off is the sudden death of one kind of plant. The dying bamboo plants drop seeds. The seeds will grow into new plants. But many years pass before the bamboo grows big enough to eat.

Giant pandas used to move to a different place after a bamboo die-off. Then they could find another kind of bamboo. But much of the forest in China has been made into farms and towns. Only one kind of bamboo grows on each mountain. After a bamboo die-off, many giant pandas starve. Starve means to suffer or die from lack of food.

Bamboo die-offs have happened several times. People in China try to help the giant pandas during a die-off. They bring other kinds of bamboo into the forests. Then the giant pandas have food to eat.

Giant pandas eat 15 kinds of bamboo.

Giant Pandas and People

Giant pandas are an endangered species. Endangered means in danger of dying out. A species is a kind of animal. There are only about 700 to 1,000 giant pandas in the world. About 70 giant pandas live in zoos in China and other countries.

People are trying to save the giant pandas. China has set aside 12 large areas of land for giant pandas. These areas are called giant panda reserves. People study giant pandas there to learn more about them. Guards protect them from hunters. Anyone who kills a giant panda there is sent to prison.

The Chinese government rewards people who help giant pandas. The government is trying to turn some farmland back into bamboo forest. Giant pandas could then find more bamboo after a die-off. Many people are working to save the giant pandas.

There are only 700 to 1,000 giant pandas in the world.

Fast Facts

Common Name: Giant panda

Scientific name: Ailuropoda melanoleuca

Life span: Up to 30 years in zoos

Height: Adult male giant pandas are five to six feet (more than one and one half meters) long from nose to tail. Females are a little shorter.

Weight: Cubs weigh about four ounces (112 grams) at birth. Adult males weigh 175 to 275 pounds (80 to 125 kilograms). Adult females weigh a little less.

Features: Giant pandas have thick white and black fur. Each front foot has a panda's thumb. This is a long part of the wristbone that is used like a thumb.

Population: Scientists believe there are only 700 to 1,000 pandas in the world. About 70 live in zoos.

Home: Giant pandas live in bamboo forests in the mountains of western China.

Diet: Giant pandas eat mainly the stems and leaves of bamboo plants. They sometimes eat other plants, small animals, or fish.

Words to Know

bamboo (bam-BOO)—a tall grass with tough stems
die-off (DYE-off)—when every plant of a species dies and drops seeds
endangered (ehn-DAYN-jehrd)—in danger of dying out
habitat (HA-bih-tat)—the place where an animal makes its home
mate (MAIT)—to join together to produce young
reserve (ree-ZURV)—an area of land set aside for animals to use

Read More

Arnold, Caroline. *Panda.* New York: Morrow, 1992.
Lee, Sandra. *Giant Panda.* New York: The Child's World, 1993.
Wong, Ovid K. *Giant Pandas.* Chicago: Children's Press, 1987.

Useful Addresses

World Wildlife Fund
1250 24th St. NW
P.O. Box 96555
Washington, D.C. 20077-
7795

Busch Gardens
P.O. Box 9158
Tampa, FL 33674

Internet Sites

Electronic Zoo
http://netvet.wustl.edu/e-zoo.htm
ZooNet
http://www.mindspring.com/~zoonet/

Index

bamboo, 5, 7, 9, 11, 13, 19, 21
China, 5, 9, 13, 19, 21
cub, 17
die-off, 19, 21
endangered, 21
fur, 7
hunting, 13, 21
leopard, 13

mating, 15
panda's thumbs, 7
population, 21
predators, 13
range, 9
reserves, 21
weight, 5, 17
zoos, 21